Early American Patchwork Quilt Designs

SUSAN JOHNSTON

Dover Publications, Inc.
New York

Publisher's Note

Cherry Basket, Milky Way, Jack in the Box, Cats and Mice—these are among the concrete objects that have lent their names to the geometric abstractions of standard pieced quilt blocks. Some of the blocks evolved in the Old World and crossed with the colonists to the New. Others are grounded in the new land and its influences, notably Indian design. Unique to America is the way in which the blocks are used—the block style: the same block is repeated in rows down and across the quilt surface, rather than functioning as a border motif mixed with other such elements encircling a central medallion, in the European manner. Sometimes the blocks are isolated from each other by strips, called sashes, spaced between; other times the blocks touch and the geometry interlocks. Borders are optional and, when present, either simple or elaborate. The dominant design element is block repetition and interplay.

The finished patchwork quilt is itself known as "a Merry Go Round" or "a Susannah": identity and continuity rest in the blocks. After all, quilts themselves are perishable. Although many were constructed, not one survives from the seventeenth century; and while there are today quilts from the eighteenth and nineteenth centuries, millions more were made and used until they wore out. Among patchwork, or pieced, quilts, the casualty rate was particularly high. The result of a technique considered simple enough for young, inexperienced fingers and old, failing eyes, pieced quilts were not treasured as masterworks. Relying on patchwork to meet the everyday need for warm bedcovers, the needleworker turned to appliqué and embroidery to display her skills in "best" or "show" quilts. Skills went into piecing nonetheless, not least among them a sense of form and color, and created the individual design experiment embodied in each early American patchwork quilt.

Now you may participate in the experiment. Choosing among the riches contained in hundreds of different traditional blocks, Susan Johnston has selected 42 and used them in the block style (with the exception of number 41, a medallion with block border) to create 42 early American patchwork quilt designs. The individual blocks used to make these quilts have been reproduced for you on the final pages of the book. If you wish to add color, the examples on the covers, rendered in colors seen in surviving American quilts, will guide you to a traditional look. Have fun exercising your own design sense within a venerable folk medium.

Published in Canada by General Publishing Company, Ltd., 30 Lesmill Road, Don Mills, Toronto, Ontario.
Published in the United Kingdom by Constable and Company, Ltd., 10 Orange Street, London WC2H 7EG.

Early American Patchwork Quilt Designs, as published by Dover Publications, Inc., in 1986, is a slightly revised publication incorporating all the designs of the work originally published by Dover in 1984 under the title *Early American Patchwork Quilts to Color*.

DOVER *Pictorial Archive* SERIES

International Standard Book Number: 0-486-24583-7

Manufactured in the United States of America
Dover Publications, Inc., 31 East 2nd Street, Mineola, N.Y. 11501

1. BASKET OF SCRAPS

2. ECHO LOG CABIN (HUNG)

3. STRAWBERRY

4. ALL KINDS

5. SUNFLOWER STAR

6. BUILDING STAR

7. GRAPE BASKET

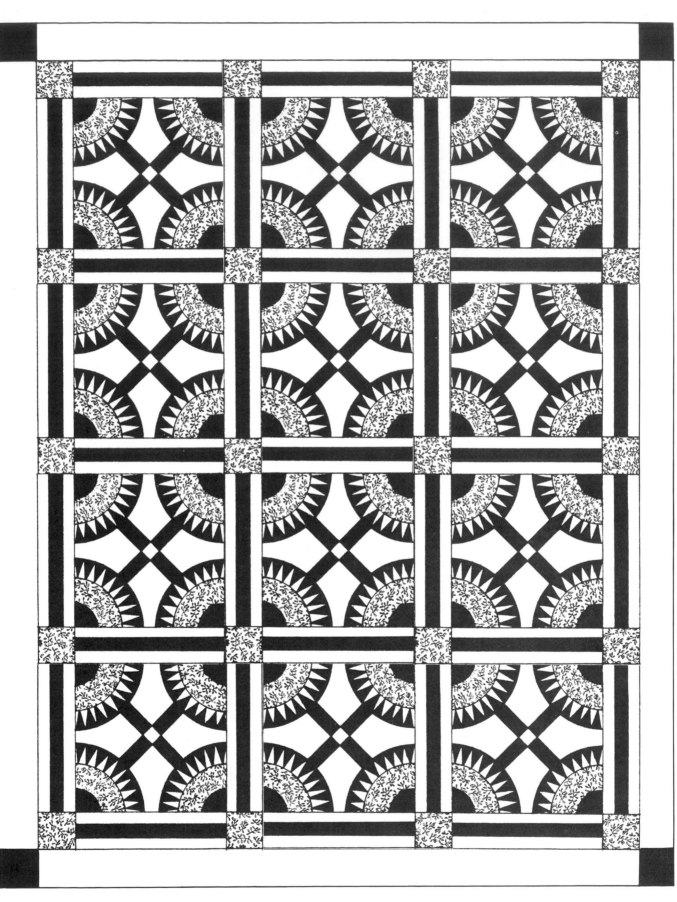

8. SPLIT RAIL

9. PINWHEEL (1)

10. CLOCKWORKS

11. SUGAR LOAF

12.　1893 WORLD'S FAIR

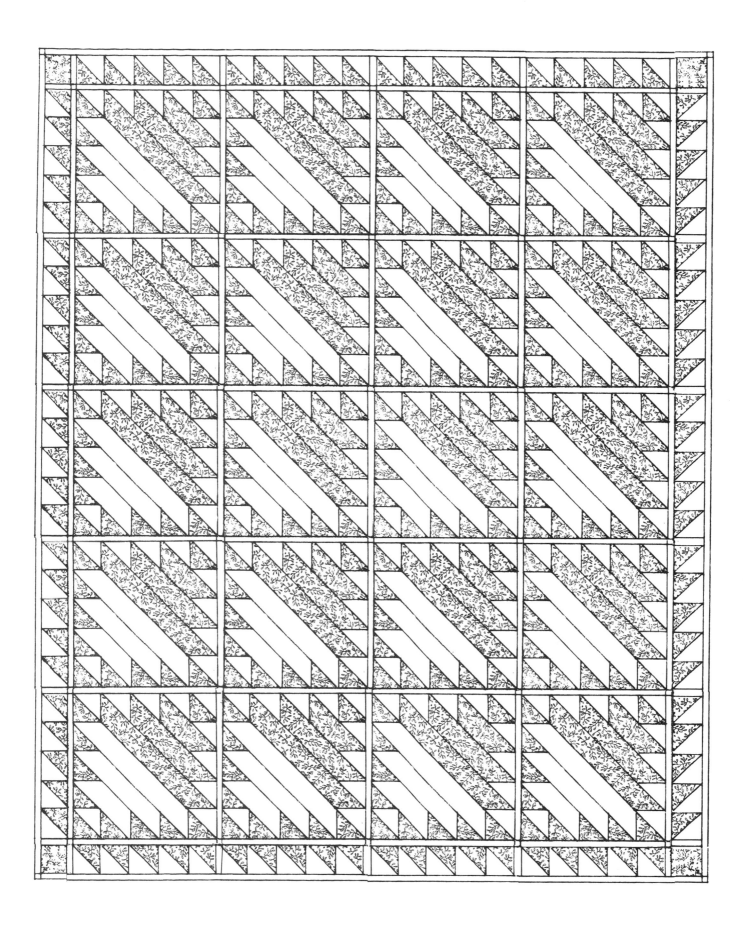

13. LADY OF THE LAKE

14.   CROSS AND CROWN

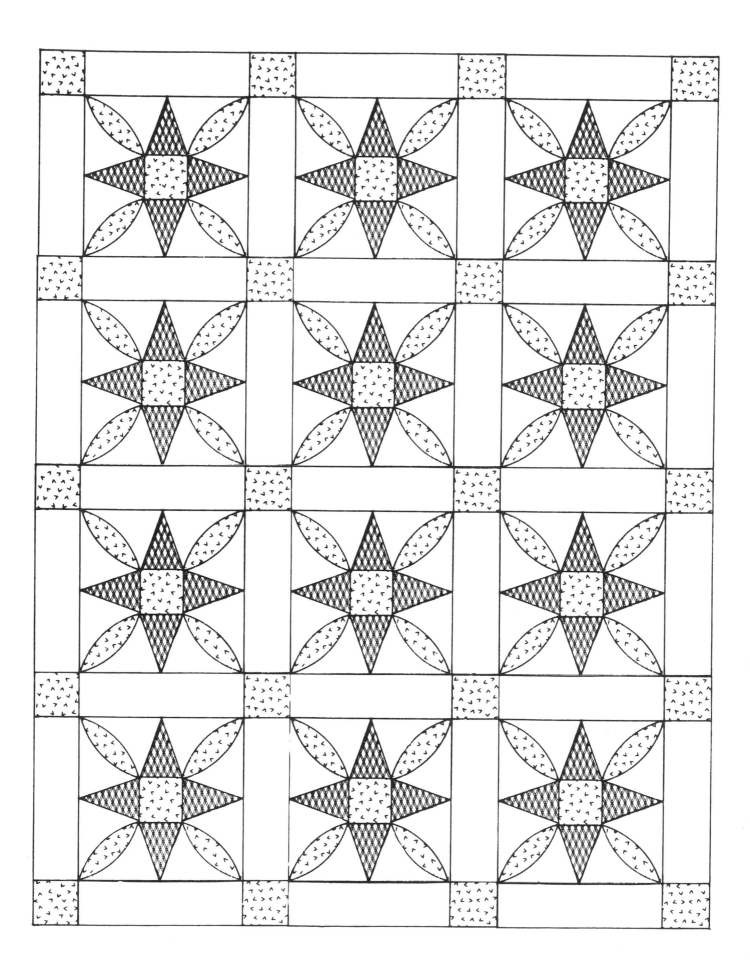

15.   MORNING STAR

16. KING'S CROWN

17. NECKTIE

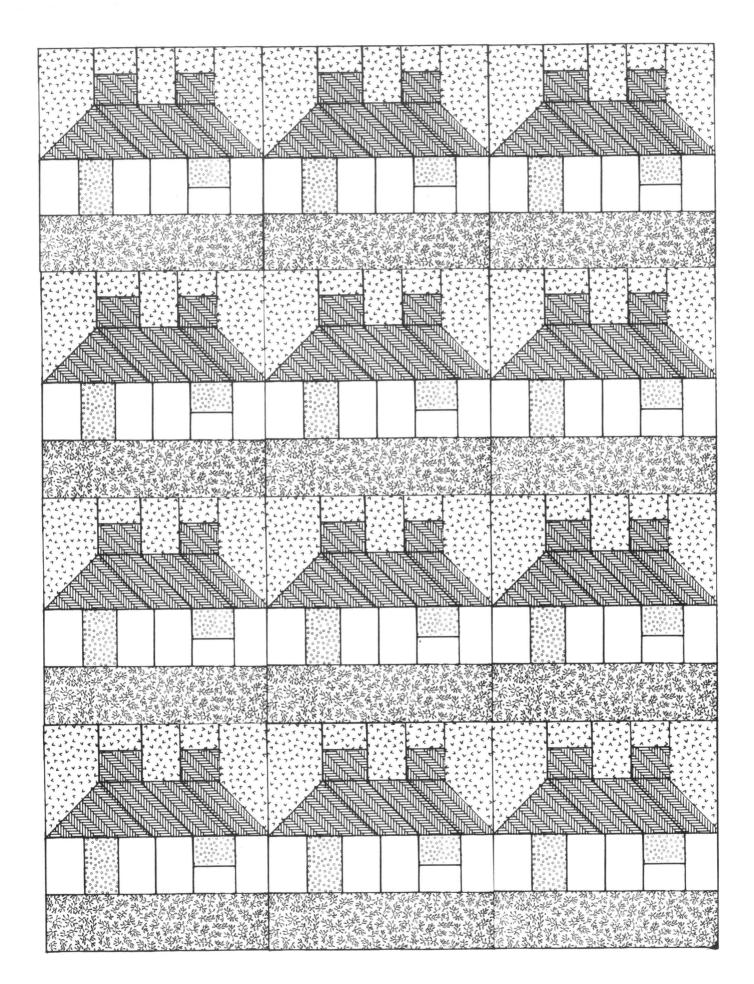

18. HOUSE ON THE HILL

19. SUSANNAH

20. HANDS ALL ROUND

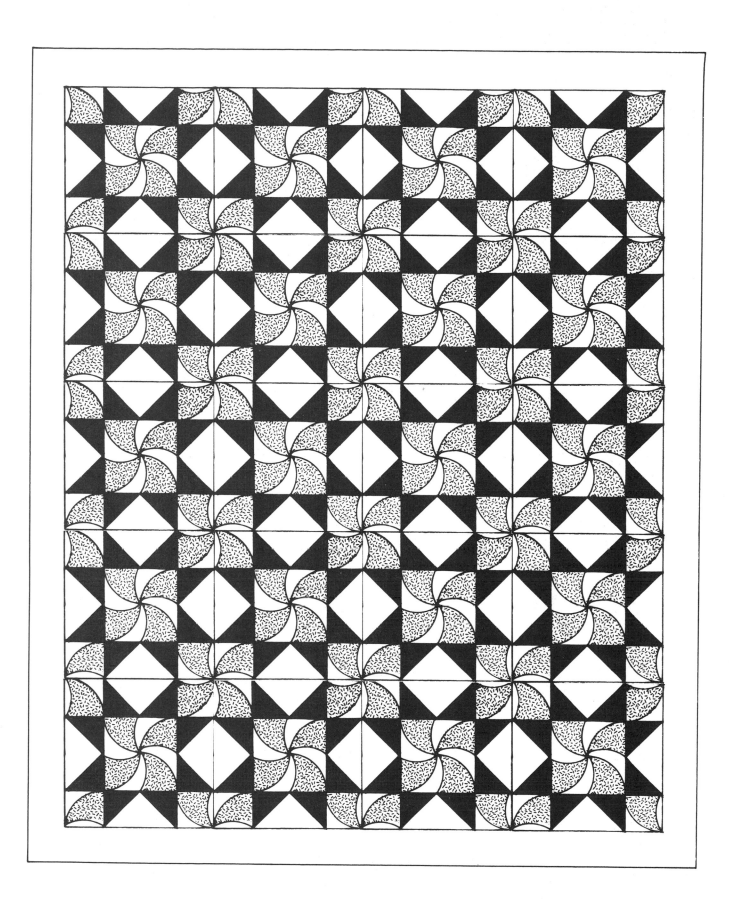

21. PINWHEEL (2)

22. CHERRY BASKET

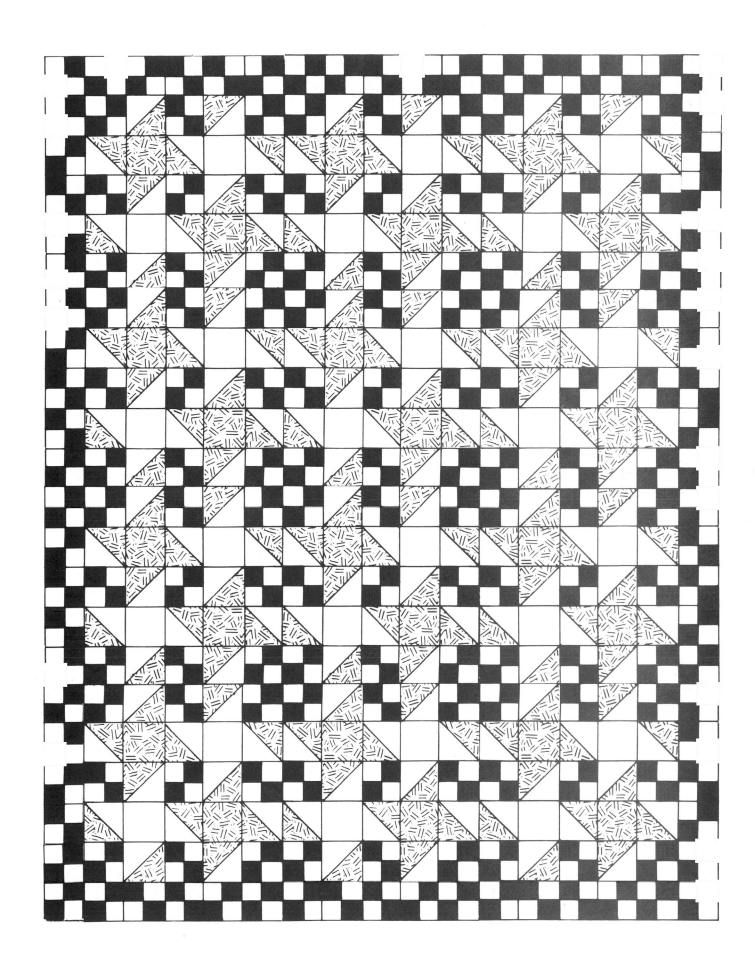

23. MILKY WAY

24. MILADY'S FAN

25. PALM LEAVES HOSANNAH

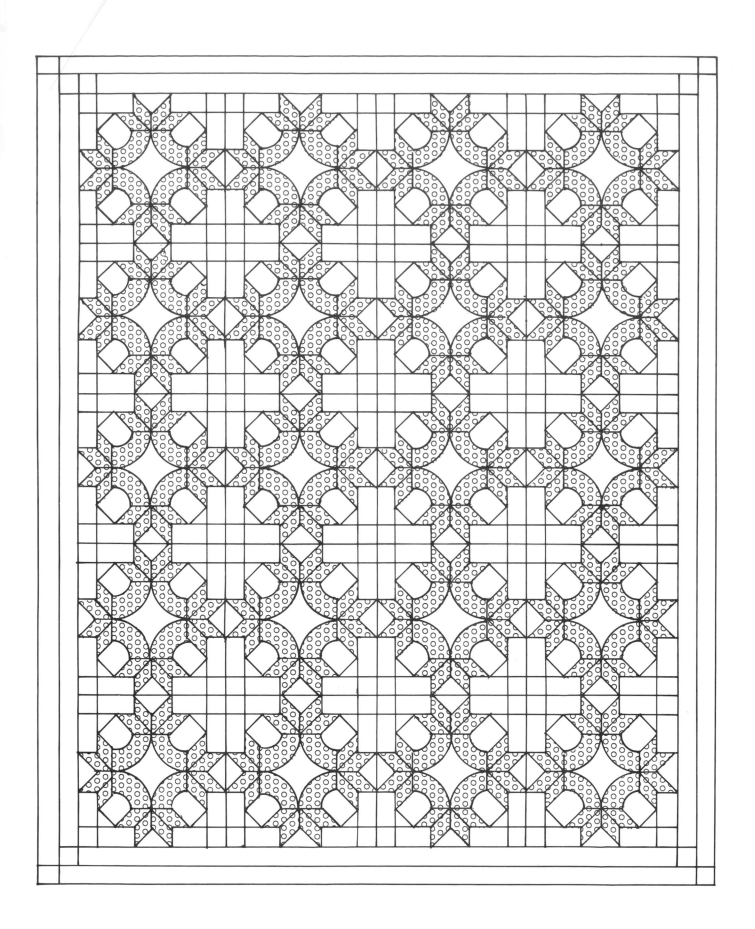

26.   FRIENDSHIP KNOT

27. OCEAN WAVE

28. STARRY PATH

29. FRENCH STAR

30. MAPLE LEAF

31. OLD TIPPECANOE VARIATION

32. CATS AND MICE

33. MERRY GO ROUND

34. V BLOCK

35.　IRISH CHAIN QUILT

36. CRAZY ANN

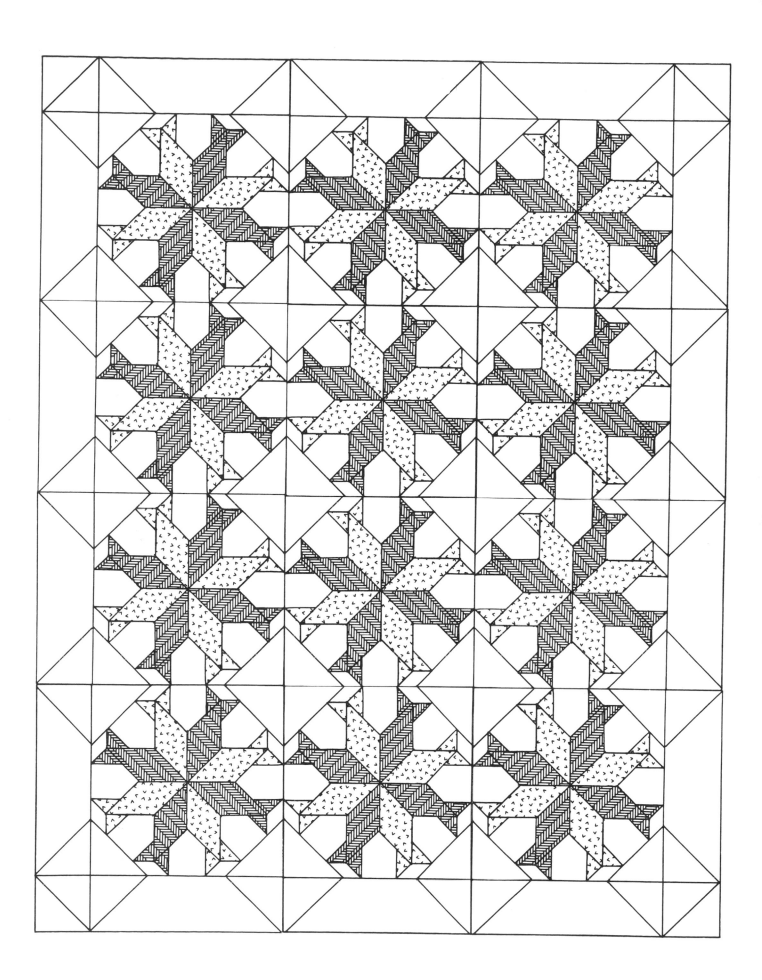

37. FISH BLOCK

38. MONKEY WRENCH

39. MARY TENNY GREY TRAVEL CLUB

40. JACK IN THE BOX

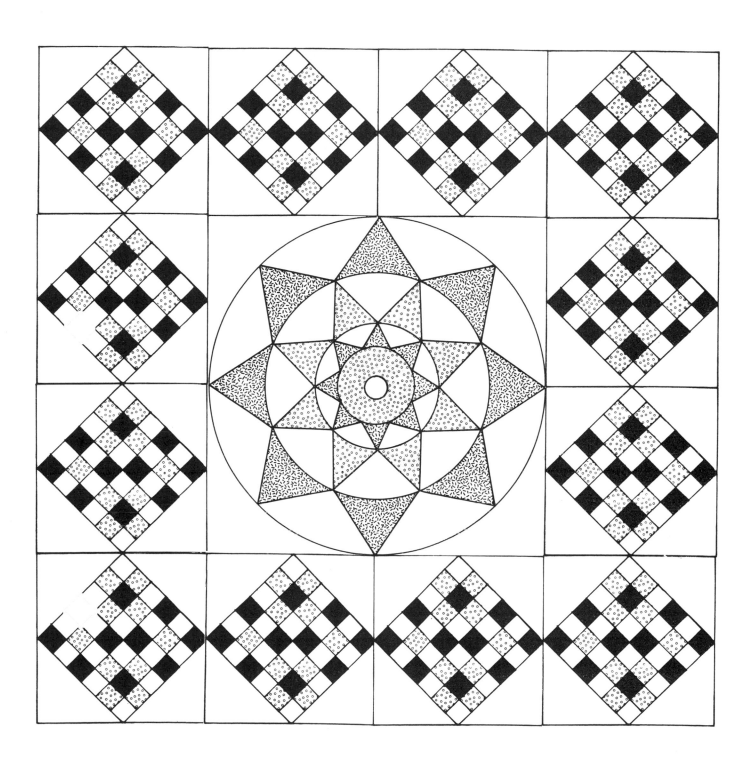

41. SUNBURST MEDALLION

42. MARTHA WASHINGTON STAR

Quilt Blocks

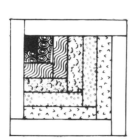

1. BASKET OF SCRAPS

2. ECHO LOG CABIN (HUNG)

3. STRAWBERRY

4. ALL KINDS

5. SUNFLOWER STAR

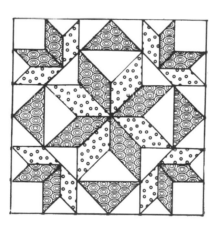

6. BUILDING STAR

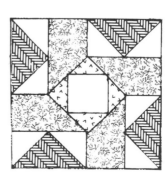

7. GRAPE BASKET

8. SPLIT RAIL

9. PINWHEEL (1)

10. CLOCKWORKS

11. SUGAR LOAF

12. 1893 WORLD'S FAIR

13. LADY OF THE LAKE

14. CROSS AND CROWN

15. MORNING STAR

16. KING'S CROWN

17. NECKTIE

18. HOUSE ON THE HILL

19. SUSANNAH

20. HANDS ALL ROUND

21. PINWHEEL (2)

22. CHERRY BASKET

23. MILKY WAY

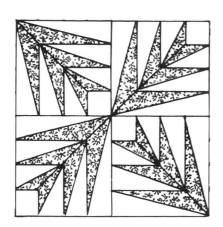

25. PALM LEAVES HOSANNAH

24. MILADY'S FAN

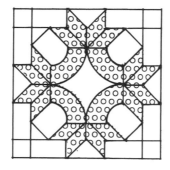

26. FRIENDSHIP KNOT

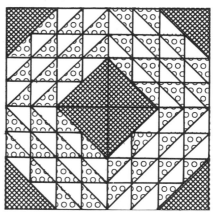

27. OCEAN WAVE

28. STARRY PATH

29. FRENCH STAR

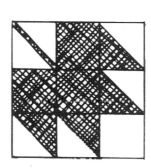

30. MAPLE LEAF

31. OLD TIPPECANOE VARIATION

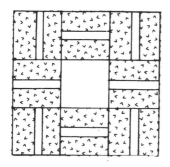

32. CATS AND MICE

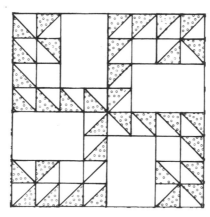

33. MERRY GO ROUND

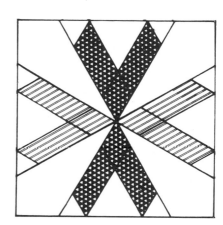

34. V BLOCK

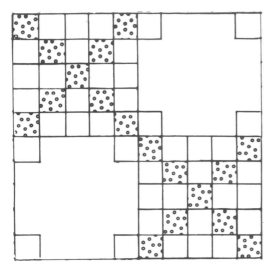

35. IRISH CHAIN QUILT

36. CRAZY ANN

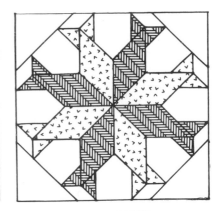

37. FISH BLOCK

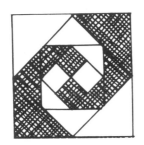

38. MONKEY WRENCH

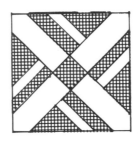

39. MARY TENNY GREY TRAVEL CLUB

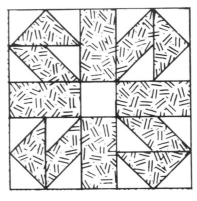

40. JACK IN THE BOX

41. SUNBURST MEDALLION

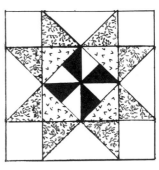

42. MARTHA WASHINGTON STAR